GANDHI

Reference Edition Published 1988

Published by Marshall Cavendish Corporation
147 West Merrick Road
Freeport, Long Island
N.Y. 11520

Printed in Italy by New Interlitho, Milan.

Designed and produced by
AS Publishing

Library of Congrass Cataloging-in-Publication Data

Gandhi.
      p. cm—(Children of history; 4)
    Includes index.
    Summary: A childhood biography of the Indian nationalist leader
who followed a doctrine of nonviolent civil disobedience.
    ISBN 0-86307-926-1. ISBN 0-86307-922-9 (set)
    1. Gandhi, Mahatma, 1869-1948—Childhood and youth—Juvenile
literature. 2. Statesmen—India—Biography—Juvenile literature.
3. Nationalists—India—Biography—Juvenile literature.
[1. Gandhi, Mahatma, 1969-1948—Childhood and youth. 2. Statesmen.]
I. Series: Children of history; v. 4.
DS481.G3G21672 1988
954.03'5'0924—dc19
[B]
[92]

CHILDREN OF HISTORY

GANDHI

By Brenda Clarke
Illustrated by Roger Payne

MARSHALL CAVENDISH
NEW YORK, LONDON, TORONTO

**Young Mohandas watches
an elephant parade with his
mother and father. As
diwan, his father was the
most important citizen in
Porbandar, next to the
prince.**

The Gandhi Family

Each afternoon as school closed in the Indian town where
he lived, a small figure could be seen running home alone
through the hot, dusty streets. Each morning, the same
small boy retraced his steps slowly, dragging his feet to
make sure that he arrived at school at the very last moment
before lessons began. The boy, Mohandas Karamchand
Gandhi, went to great lengths to avoid meeting other pupils
out of school. His shyness made him terrified of having to
talk to them, let alone join them in their games. Only at
home with his family did he feel safe and happy.

Yet, years later, this same nervous little boy had grown so
strong in his beliefs that he had the courage to challenge the
might of the British Empire and lead his country, India, on
the path to independence from British rule.

A Political Family

Young Mohandas came from a large family. His father had
married four times, although his first three wives died while
still young. From these early marriages, Mr. Gandhi had
two daughters. His fourth wife, Putlibai, had a daughter
and three sons. The youngest child, born on October 2,
1869, was Mohandas.

Mohandas's father, Karamchand Uttamchand Gandhi,
was an important man in the small town of Porbandar. He
was the chief minister, or diwan. Porbandar is a city on the
west coast of India. Today it is part of the large state of
Gujarat, but when Mohandas was born it formed a separate
state. In those days, there were hundreds of such small
states in India, each ruled by a royal prince, under the
protection of the British Empire. Day to day running of the
state was left to the prince and his ministers.

HINDU BELIEF AND CUSTOMS

Hindus believe in one Supreme Spirit, or God, called Brahman. This Spirit is shown in many different forms – male or female, human or animal, or half-human and half-animal.

Hindu society is divided into classes, or castes, called *varna*. At the top are priests, or *Brahmins*. Next come warriors or rulers, the *Kshatrivas*. Third are the *Vaishyas*, the merchants and traders. To this caste the Gandhis belonged. Lastly come the craftsmen, or *Shudras*. Below all these are the outcasts or "Untouchables". By tradition they were given the dirtiest jobs and suffered prejudice and discrimination. Gandhi tried to change people's attitude towards them and called them *harijans*, "children of God".

At Home with the Family

Mohandas's father had little formal education, but he was a skilled administrator and knew how to cope with the different problems brought to him by the prince, the citizens of Porbandar and the officials of the British government. A member of the Gandhi family had held the position of diwan for many years, and Mr. Gandhi hoped that a son of his would one day succeed him in the office.

The Gandhis were a religious family, followers of the Hindu god Vishnu. They were strict in their practice, eating no meat and drinking no alcohol. Mohandas's mother was particularly religious, with a strong regard for truth and goodness. Mohandas loved and respected his father, but it was from his mother that he learned the importance of kindness and self-sacrifice.

His Mother's Example

The family shared their three-story home with Mr. Gandhi's five brothers, their wives and children, so there were always plenty of cousins for the young Gandhis to play with. Mrs Gandhi often found herself looking after not only her own children, but her nieces and nephews too. She was patient, gentle and cheerful, allowing them to play around her as she worked. Sometimes she stopped her housework to tell them stories. Young Mohandas loved to sit with his cousins, listening to his mother as she told them tales of the god Vishnu and his wife Lakshmi.

Mohandas's aunts would also take their turns caring for the children, but if anyone was ill it was always Mohandas's mother who looked after them. She was indispensable as a nurse. She would watch over her patient night and day, unstinting in her care, until she herself was quite worn out. She always put the welfare of others before her own.

In this, as in so much else, Mohandas followed her example. In later years he helped to nurse his aging father and, when living in South Africa, he organized an ambulance service to care for wounded soldiers. When plague broke out in the poor Indian quarter of Johannesburg, he stayed by the bedsides of the sufferers, bringing them comfort regardless of his own safety.

All the children in the Gandhi household loved listening to stories. A Brahmin teacher used to visit the house to teach them holy scriptures, but they preferred listening to tales of the gods told to them by Mrs. Gandhi.

Lessons for Life

Mohandas's mother was an intelligent woman. As wife of the diwan, she was well acquainted with politics. Her husband's position meant that the family was comfortably off, although not wealthy. But Putlibai cared little for possessions, fine clothes or jewelry. She spent as much time as she could spare from her domestic duties in worship and prayer at the nearby temple. As a devout Vaishnava Hindu she believed in non-violence to all living things (*ahimsa*). Like the rest of her family, she never ate meat. Sometimes she ate nothing at all, for her religion also taught that fasting aided self-discipline and purification.

Looking for the Sunshine

Mohandas had a strong childhood memory of his mother's fasts. One year, during the long season of monsoon rains, Mrs. Gandhi took a vow not to eat each day before seeing the sun. At this time of the year the sky was often overcast all day. Mohandas joined his sisters, brothers and cousins on watch outside, waiting anxiously for a glimpse of sunlight. When it came, they called urgently for Putlibai to come quickly, see the sun, and so be able to eat a meal. If the sun failed to shine, or if Putlibai came too late to see it, she took this as a sign that her fast was to last all day.

Fasting for Peace

In his adult life, Mohandas too found spiritual strength through fasting. He also used fasting in a different way, as a non-violent method of persuading people to give in to his political demands. While in prison in 1932, he fasted in protest against voting arrangements for Indians proposed by the British government. At the time of Indian indepen-

The Gandhi children took turns to watch for the sun during the monsoon and called their mother when it appeared. Seeing the sun meant that she could break her fast. Meanwhile she worked at her chores indoors. Mohandas's family lived on the ground floor of the house they shared with their relatives.

dence in 1947, his fasts succeeded in ending riots in the cities of Calcutta and Delhi.

Telling the Truth

Keeping to the standards of behavior he learned at home sometimes created difficulties for Mohandas. Being absolutely truthful and honest made him unpopular when it meant informing on a fellow-pupil who had misbehaved or broken school rules. But if a teacher asked him outright to name the culprit responsible for wrongdoing, Mohandas did what he knew to be right. He told the truth.

THE MONSOON
Life in India, particularly for farmers, depends upon the summer monsoons. These rain-bearing winds first blow in from the Arabian Sea in June and last until October. From October to March the monsoon changes direction to blow cool, dry winds over the country.

A Joyful Festival

Religious festivals played a large part in the lives of the young Gandhis. At least once a year their own temple had a festival and they watched, or took part in, the colorful procession which made its way around the town. The event they all looked forward to for weeks beforehand was the New Year festival of Diwali, dedicated to Vishnu and Lakshmi. In honor of this festival, celebrated towards the end of October, there was a public holiday, and time off from school.

Celebrating Diwali

Diwali was particularly important to the Gandhis and to the merchants and businessmen of their caste. Each day of the festival is celebrated in a different way. One day is set aside for men to visit their sisters, to enjoy a meal with them and honor them with presents. Another commemorates Vishnu's victory over the demon Naraka. A third day, dedicated to Lakshmi, goddess of wealth and good fortune, marks the beginning of the new business year. On this day, account books for the past year are offered to the goddess, together with gold, silver and money, with prayers for success in the financial year to come.

The young Gandhis enjoyed themselves enormously during Diwali, paying visits and exchanging gifts. Their house would be hung with decorations, feasts were prepared, and new clothes made ready for wearing. But for the children, nothing could equal the excitement of night time, when they lit little earthenware lamps of oil and set them down outside the house to shed light all around. Mohandas was enchanted. Everywhere he looked, lights flickered and winked – from every house front, from the temple, through the trees, and from the river.

At the festival of Diwali, Mohandas joined his family with the crowds in the streets. Lamps were alight throughout the town and even on the river. Mohandas gazed entranced at the flickering lights, but held on tight to his mother's hand as the fireworks crackled and exploded in the darkness.

Easily Led

As a child, Mohandas did not question what older people told him. He accepted what parents and teachers said, holding always to the cardinal rules of truth and duty. His passive nature, however, could lead him into trouble.

When he was about six years old, Mohandas and his cousins found themselves one day with nothing much to do. They wandered towards the temple, where there was usually something of interest happening. But today the temple seemed deserted. Nobody was about, not even a temple priest. The boys hung around the courtyard, and

Startled from his nap by a sudden noise, the temple priest surprises Mohandas and his friends as they run away, dropping the statues they have stolen. Mohandas, in shame, knew he must own up to his part in the escapade.

then decided to take a look inside the building. It too was empty, and gloomy compared with the sunny yard outside. Their eyes fixed on the lights burning before the temple statues of Vishnu and Lakshmi, turning the bronze images into shining gold.

Offending the Gods

The older boys crept towards the figure of Vishnu, while Mohandas held back, hesitating nervously. Then he ran to follow them. He was frightened of being left behind in the darkness. But he was frightened too of approaching the sacred images. As he caught up with his companions, the boldest of the cousins reached out and grasped the statue. Mohandas was horrified. The god would be so angry.

The older boys, stifling giggles, ran in all directions around the temple, picking up as many small statues as they could carry. Then they made for the door. But as they ran, one of the images fell with a clang to the floor. For a moment they stood still, and then, from within, they heard approaching footsteps. They fled: out through the doorway and across the temple courtyard.

Owning Up

Before they could reach the safety of the street, a panting priest caught up with them. Angrily, he demanded to know what they were doing. The older boys looked shamefacedly at the ground. Nobody spoke. Again the priest asked them.

Little Mohandas, trembling with fear, bit his lip and swallowed hard. He was going to cry. What would his mother say? He had been so bad. Even as he wondered, he knew what his mother would want him to do. He must tell the truth now, and own up. So, in breathless gulps, he confessed to the outraged priest what they had done.

The god Vishnu is one of the three main Hindu gods. He is called "the Preserver" and is pictured carrying a lotus flower, a conch shell, a magical discus to use as a weapon, and a mace. His wife Lakshmi bestows gifts of coins. She is always shown on a lotus blossom with lotus flowers in her hands.

The Young Schoolboy

Mohandas learned his early lessons at home, mainly in the form of stories from the Hindu scriptures told to him by his mother or his nurse, Rambha. Later he had a teacher, a Brahmin priest who helped him learn the holy texts of Vishnu.

As soon as he was old enough, he was sent to the local primary school in Porbandar, but he could remember learning little there. In such a small town, the school was poorly equipped and beginners had to learn their Gujarati alphabet while sitting outside in the sun, writing in the dust with their fingers.

Apart from mastering multiplication tables, which he found difficult, the only achievement Gandhi remembered from these early schooldays was learning from the other boys all sorts of names to call the teacher! This, he thought, suggested that "my intellect must have been sluggish and my memory raw".

A New School

At the age of seven, Mohandas and his family moved from Porbandar. Mr. Gandhi had a new position as diwan of Rajkot, a state further inland. In Rajkot there was a high school, and here Mohandas began his education in earnest.

The shy young Mohandas found school hard. He could not bear to talk to his new schoolfellows, fearing they would poke fun at him for his thin legs, or his clumsiness, or his large ears. He ran home every day to escape their company. He did not excel at schoolwork, either. Reports in most subjects described him as just about average: "good at English, fair at Arithmetic and weak in Geography: conduct very good; bad handwriting".

LEARNING THE LANGUAGE
The land of India which Britain ruled was vast and varied. Some states were rich because the land was fertile, others were poor. People from different states had different customs and traditions. There were many different languages. The language of northwest India, where the Gandhis lived, was Gujarati. Young Mohandas learned to write his letters at the local school in Porbandar. He did not learn fluent English until much later, when studying to be a lawyer.

Under Inspection

During his first year at Rajkot, a school inspector came to visit. Mohandas's teacher was anxious that his pupils should impress. The inspector set a spelling test for the class, giving them five words to write down.

One word was "kettle", and the nervous Mohandas made a mistake as he scrawled it on his slate. Seeing his pupil's error, the teacher slyly tapped him with his foot, trying to prompt Mohandas to look at his neighbor's work. Mohandas took no notice. His teacher thought him too slow to understand the hint that he should copy his neighbor's correct spelling. But the problem was not that Mohandas was "too slow". It was just that the idea of cheating would never have occurred to him.

At high school, Mohandas had a desk to sit at and a slate to write on. When the school inspector came to visit, the teacher wanted his class to make a good impression. He even wanted Mohandas to copy the right answers from another boy!

A Fearful Nature

Mohandas did not distinguish himself on the sports field either. This was partly because of his small physique and awkwardness, but also because of his anxious, fearful nature. Even boys smaller than himself could terrify him. So while school games were in progress, he much preferred to find a quiet spot where he could read or, if he could, wander away unnoticed.

Poor Mohandas was afraid of so many things: "I used to be haunted by the fear of thieves, ghosts and serpents. I did not dare to stir out of doors at night. Darkness was a terror to me. It was almost impossible for me to sleep in the dark as I would imagine ghosts coming from one direction, thieves from another, and serpents from a third. I could not therefore bear to sleep without a light in the room".

The Mantra's Aid

Mohandas was ashamed of his fears, and tried hard to overcome them. He had a powerful desire to make himself strong. His old nurse Rambha had reassured him and given him some advice. There was nothing wrong in admitting his fear, she said, but when he felt threatened by anything he should not run away from it. Instead he should stand his ground and repeat a sacred text, or *mantra*, over and over again in his head.

By repeating his mantra – *Rama, Rama, Rama,* – he could turn fear into fearlessness. The mantra would make his mind steady and calm, so that nothing could shake him from his goal. For a while Mohandas tried this, to please Rambha, but being only a boy he soon forgot about it. Later in life, however, the mantra came back to him, and became a great source of strength whenever he faced political conflict and physical danger.

Self-Improvement

Mohandas dreamed of being brave like the Hindu heroes he read about in his books. These included Harischandra and Prahlada, the legendary examples of truthfulness and sacrifice. King Harischandra gave up all he had for the sake of truth, while the boy Prahlada suffered untold hardships without faltering in his faith in God. Gandhi's model for obedience to his parents and elders came from the story of Shrava, who carried his blind parents on a religious pilgrimage.

Mohandas tried hard to put these ideals into practice at home. He helped his mother with her household chores and joined her in nursing his father, who was becoming weakened by illness.

At Gandhi's high school, all the senior boys had to play games. Gandhi disliked sports and preferred reading to cricket. Once he missed a gymnastics class when nursing his sick father. The headmaster did not believe his excuse and accused him of lying. This made Mohandas very upset. The Gandhis never told lies.

Getting Married

At the age of 13, Mohandas took a year off from school to be married. When he was seven, his parents had, according to custom, betrothed him to a girl of the same caste who was considered a suitable bride for him. Mr. and Mrs. Gandhi had previously selected two other brides, but they had died before they were old enough to marry. The third choice for Mohandas was the daughter of a merchant from Porbandar. She was the same age as her future husband and her name was Kasturbai Makanji.

A Family Affair

Hindu weddings are splendid, costly affairs which take many months to prepare. In order to make the most of the time and money spent on the arrangements, the Gandhis decided that Mohandas's older brother Karsandas would be married at the same time, along with one of their cousins.

On their wedding day, Mohandas and Kasturbai appeared at the ceremony in their new clothes, wearing flower garlands around their necks. The couple were showered with rice grains, exchanged their garlands and, with the guests, offered prayers before a sacred fire. Priests chanted while the couple took seven steps around the fire, asking for wealth, healthy children and a long life. Then, the ceremony over, bride and groom joined the guests in the general fun and feasting.

For Mohandas's brother and cousin, marriage meant the end of their education. Mohandas was luckier. He went back to school, but often found himself thinking of his pretty young wife while he tried to work. He was jealously fond of her, and taking his responsibilities seriously, felt that he must educate her and teach her how to be an ideal wife. But Kasturbai had a mind and a will of her own.

CHILD MARRIAGE
Indian marriages were usually arranged between families, often when the boy and girl involved were small children. After their wedding, Mohandas and Kasturbai did not live together all the time. While he continued his school studies, she went back to her parents' home. Later, Gandhi spoke out against child marriage, believing it to be wrong.

Like all Hindu weddings, Mohandas's marriage to Kasturbai was a colorful ceremony. The evening after a Hindu marriage, the young couple look at the Pole Star together, vowing to be as firm and constant in their marriage as the star in the sky.

19

Teenage Rebellion

Now, more than ever, Mohandas felt ashamed of his secret fears. He knew that the dark held no terrors for Kasturbai, who would happily go anywhere at night, untroubled by thoughts of lurking serpents or ghosts.

By this time Mohandas was at the high school at Katyavar, where among his few friends was a Muslim boy called Sheikh Mehtab. Mehtab knew how much Mohandas wanted to be strong like him. The difference between them, Mehtab explained, was that Mohandas never ate meat. He should follow the example of the British, who were tall, brave and strong because they fed on meat. Eventually Mohandas agreed to an experiment.

Guilty Secrets

The two boys met at a lonely spot near the river, and here Mohandas tasted meat for the first time. It was goat's flesh, and tough, and it made him feel sick. It also gave him nightmares, in which he dreamt that a live goat was bleating inside him. Nevertheless, he tried meat again several times. Then he grew so conscience-stricken at inventing stories to explain his lack of appetite at dinner that he gave up the experiments.

For a while, Mohandas also took up smoking in secret. He and a cousin collected cigarette butts thrown away by his uncle. But the supply soon ran out and in order to buy their own cigarettes, Mohandas and his cousin pilfered pennies from their servants. If nothing else was available, they even tried smoking stalks from wild plants! Feeling that the situation was out of hand, the boys thought of suicide – but finally decided simply to give up smoking. Mohandas knew that his behavior was wrong, and vowed to himself "never again".

His Father's Forgiveness

Only once did Mohandas break his own rules, by stealing some gold from his brother in order to pay off the brother's debts. Mohandas still felt enormous guilt about what he had done and wrote a confession to his father. After reading it, father and son were both so overcome that they wept. Karamchand forgave his son readily, and Mohandas never stole again.

Mr. Gandhi's health was steadily failing, and towards the end of his life he became bedridden. Mohandas tended his father whenever he could, massaging his legs at night to make him more comfortable. But when Mohandas was 16, his father died.

Mohandas and his cousin smoked their cigarettes in the open air, in places where nobody would recognize them. At the polo field they saw a visiting team of British officers enjoying refreshments with their wives during a game. The polo players looked big and strong to Mohandas; his friend told him he too could grow tall and sturdy if he would eat meat.

The Young Lawyer

In 1887 Mohandas became a student at Samaldas College in Bhavnagar, having just managed to pass his entrance exams. Here another difficulty arose. The lectures were given not in Gujarati but in English, which Mohandas found hard to follow. He had some idea of becoming a doctor, but after five months of failing in every class, he left college and went home.

Going to England

One of his uncles now suggested that Mohandas should study law in England. Mohandas liked the idea, but felt sad at leaving his mother, wife and baby son. His only other trips from home had been by bullock cart to nearby towns. Mr. Gandhi had left little money and it seemed as if Kasturbai's jewelry would have to be sold until one of Mohandas's brothers agreed to pay his expenses.

Mohandas encountered other difficulties. He traveled by cart and camel to Porbandar to seek permission for the trip from his uncle, the oldest member of the family, but his uncle viewed travel abroad as unholy. Mrs. Gandhi too had grave misgivings, but felt happier after Mohandas took a vow not to touch wine, women or meat while he was away.

Finally, as Mohandas was ready to sail, he was summoned to a meeting of elders of his caste and told that the trip broke the rules of the Hindu religion. Mohandas screwed up his courage to resist the decree of these wise men, and they decided to outlaw him from the caste. But before the order could affect him, Mohandas had left India. He sailed from Bombay on September 4, 1888. Ten days after arriving in England he joined the law college of the Inner Temple in London.

Although homesick, Mohandas was thrilled to be in the heart of London. He admired the Houses of Parliament, for he had great faith in British law and justice. But in the cold, damp climate he felt chilly and out of place in the white flannel suit he had brought from home. He felt everyone was staring at him.

23

Finding his Feet

The young Gandhi's first few months in England were wretched. Everything around him was different and new, from the damp, cold climate to the electric lights and elevators which he saw for the first time. Everything he said and did seemed to be wrong; even the clothes he wore were out of place. Lonely and homesick, he shed tears each night in his apartment at Richmond near London.

The steamship journey had itself been a great trial. He encountered Western dress, food and manners for the first

Among the members of the Vegetarian Society in London, Gandhi found friends who shared not only his diet but also some of his beliefs. They talked about the simple life, loving others, and non-violence. Gandhi wrote articles for the vegetarians' journal and spoke at their meetings.

time and often felt himself the butt of ridicule when he was misunderstood or did the wrong thing. His imperfect English made him afraid to speak to fellow-passengers, or to ask the waiters what was in the unfamiliar dishes put before him at meal times. To be sure of not touching meat, Gandhi lived on fruits and sweets he had brought with him.

Once in England, fellow students worried that his strange diet of porridge, boiled spinach and bread and jam would ruin his health. Gandhi felt hungry most of the time. Secretly he had always wanted to eat meat; the vow to his mother alone held him back. He was saved from starvation by a chance walk along Farringdon Street in London, where he stumbled upon a vegetarian restaurant. At last he had found somewhere to eat a nourishing meal, and fellow vegetarians who did not find him odd.

The English Gentleman

With new-found confidence, Gandhi decided to adapt to English life. He ordered suits from fashionable tailors, wearing them with silk shirts, stiff collars, colorful ties, a silk top hat and a gold watch chain sent from India.

He bought a violin and took lessons in music, ballroom dancing and correct speech. He started to learn French. After three months he realized how foolish all this was, especially as his brother in India was having to pay the bills. Gandhi then went to the opposite extreme and began keeping strict accounts of every penny he spent. He rented a single room, did his own cooking, walked up to 10 miles a day to save bus fares, and reduced his expenses to just £2 a month. He felt happier, healthier and self-reliant.

He worked at his studies and passed his law examinations in June 1891. He sailed for India the day after enrolling as a lawyer in the High Court, three years after leaving home.

GANDHI'S GUIDE
Gandhi's new vegetarian friends also introduced him to the *Bhagavadgita*, a Hindu holy book which he read for the first time in an English translation! He also read the Bible and was struck by the likeness of ideas he found in both books. The *Bhagavadgita* became his guide throughout life. He later said "The Gita has been a mother to me ever since I first became acquainted with it in 1889. I turn to it for guidance in every difficulty."

Home and Away Again

Gandhi's homecoming was saddened by news of his mother's death. He decided to go to Bombay to study Indian law, but when presenting his first case in court there was so overcome by nerves that he could not utter a word. He fled from the room amid loud laughter.

Gandhi returned to Rajkot, where a Muslim firm offered him a job for a year in Natal, South Africa. He jumped at the chance and in 1893 again said goodbye to Kasturbai, their little boy Harilal and their newborn son Manilal.

Insult and Injury

Gandhi worked hard at his legal job in South Africa. It was not the work that troubled him, but the way in which he was treated. Indians in South Africa were subjected to racial prejudice and insult, and Gandhi was no exception.

In court he was told to remove his turban, which he refused to do. But it was a journey from Durban to Pretoria that proved the turning-point in his life; during it, he was thrown off a train, beaten by a stagecoach driver, and refused entry to hotels reserved for "whites only".

From now on Gandhi used his legal knowledge to help the Indian workers, or "coolies", whose conditions of employment in South Africa made them little better than slaves. Then, near the end of his year's work, came news that the state government in Natal wanted to take away the right of the Indians to vote. Gandhi organized a petition against this, addressed to the British government in London, which refused to accept the Natal proposal. Nevertheless, the unjust law was passed. When in 1899 the Boer War began between Britain and the Boer settlers of South Africa, Gandhi supported the British, though he remained opposed to all violence.

Gandhi is thrown off the train at Pietermaritzburg. He never forgot that night. He made up his mind never to yield to force or to use force to win a cause.

The March to Freedom

Gandhi's fight against injustice in South Africa had made him an effective lawyer at last. He had settled in Durban, where his business prospered, and in 1896 he returned to India to collect his wife and family. The authorities in Natal tried to prevent him from landing on his return to South Africa. When, after 23 days, he was allowed off his ship he was greeted by violence and had to escape disguised as a policeman.

Passive Resistance

In 1901, as the Boer War came to an end, Gandhi went back to India for a year, but was recalled to South Africa to continue fighting for the Indians' cause. He did so through a policy called *satyagraha* ("firmness in truth").

When faced with injustice, insult or loss of human rights, the South African Indians employed "passive resistance". They refused to co-operate with the authorities, ignored laws curbing their rights and freedoms, and accepted whatever punishment resulted. Above all, their resistance was non-violent.

Gandhi himself was imprisoned for ignoring government orders. In 1913, to protest against a ruling that Hindu and Muslim marriages were not lawful, thousands of Indians took part in an illegal march. Thousands more workers went on strike, facing jail, flogging or death. Protests from India and Britain led to a law in 1914 which granted Indian settlers the rights of permanent citizens of South Africa. Gandhi sailed for home, believing his work to be done.

Quest for Truth

While in South Africa the Gandhis had been given many

In South Africa, Gandhi set up farm communities where people grew their own food, made their own clothes, and built their own homes. In India he developed a system of communes called *ashrams*, to which all were welcome, including Untouchables. Gandhi encouraged people to use the spinning wheel to make their own cotton cloth.

In India, salt was taxed by the British and people were forbidden to make their own salt. In 1930 Gandhi led a great *satyagraha* (non-violent protest) march to the sea at Dandi. On the shore he picked up a lump of salt, defying the law. He and 60,000 others, rich and poor, were arrested. But the government had to give in, inviting Gandhi to London for talks about independence.

expensive gifts. These were all sold and the money put into a fund for community service; Gandhi had no use for money or possessions. His study of Christianity, Islam and Hinduism had led him to believe that all religions were true. But it was the Hindu holy book, the *Bhagavadgita*, which became his guide and gave him the ideals of *aparigraha* (non-possession) and *samabhava* (accepting equally pain or pleasure; success or failure; victory or defeat).

Through following these ideals, Gandhi lost all fear, becoming a leader whose determination could not be shaken. And his determination was that the Indian people should rule themselves.

The Mahatma

On Gandhi's return to India, huge crowds greeted him as a hero. Gandhi spent the next few years traveling around his country, saddened by the poverty he found.

During the First World War, he helped to raise volunteers to fight for the British Empire, believing this would help achieve Indian self-government. When it did not, in March 1919, he called for a general strike to open an Indian campaign of *satyagraha*. Terrible bloodshed resulted, much to Gandhi's horror. When British troops fired on demonstrators at Amritsar, killing 400 people, Gandhi called for self-government within a year.

Independence and Assassination

In the campaigns of non-co-operation which followed, Gandhi was jailed several times; and Kasturbai died while staying with him in prison. But his protests and defiance eventually resulted in him going to London for talks on Indian self-government in 1931.

Not until August 15, 1947 was independence finally achieved and then not as Gandhi had hoped. Instead of becoming one united nation, British India was divided between Hindu India and Muslim Pakistan. Violence broke out between Hindus and Muslims and only the threat of Gandhi's fasting to death restored peace.

To some, Gandhi was "Bapu" (father); others gave him the title Mahatma (Great Soul). But not all Indians accepted Gandhi's message of harmony. At a prayer meeting on January 30, 1948 a Hindu extremist stood before the Mahatma and shot him. Gandhi died, repeating his mantra "Rama, Rama". India's first Prime Minister, Nehru, told the nation: "The light has gone out of our lives."

Gandhi wore his homespun *dhoti* (loin-cloth) even when meeting kings and prime ministers. He joked about this after taking tea at Buckingham Palace. The king, he said, wore enough for both of them!

Important Events in Gandhi's Life

1869	Born on October 2
1876	Gandhi family moves from Porbandar to Rajkot. Gandhi is betrothed
1877	Queen Victoria is proclaimed Empress of India
1887	Gandhi completes his Indian education, entering Samaldas College at Bhavnagar but leaving after one term
1888	Sails for London to train as a lawyer
1890	Tells fellow Indian students to work for 'big reforms in India'
1891	Lectures to London Vegetarian Society. Passes law exams and returns home
1893	Goes to work in South Africa as a lawyer
1894	Forms Natal Indian Congress
1896	Collects wife and family from India and meets leaders of Indian National Congress
1899	During Boer War, organizes Indian medical aid teams
1901	Returns briefly to India but is recalled to South Africa
1904	Founds weekly *Indian Opinion*; advances idea of *satyagraha* and starts Phoenix self-sufficient community
1908	Jailed for two months
1909	Writes *Indian Home Rule* Corresponds with Russian writer Leo Tolstoy
1913	Jailed again, but reaches agreement with South African leader Smuts to safeguard Indian citizens' rights. Smuts calls Gandhi a "saint".
1914-18	First World War
1915	Gandhi returns to India. Founds *ashram* at Ahmedabad
1919	Amritsar Massacre. Gandhi calls for non-co-operation with British. Urges Indians to use the spinning wheel, and himself adopts simplest garments
1922	Jailed for two years
1929	Indian National Congress calls for full independence
1930	Gandhi leads Salt March
1931	Represents Congress at Conference in London
1932	Uses fast as weapon when arrested. Identifies with Untouchable caste
1934	Resigns from Congress Party and devotes himself to village reforms
1937	Congress wins elections to new Indian parliament set up by Government of India Act
1939-45	Second World War. Gandhi opposes all violence and urges Britain to "quit India"
1942-44	Gandhi in prison. His wife dies in 1942
1946	India's independence is agreed upon. Gandhi opposes the idea of separate states for Hindus and Muslims
1947	August 15 is Independence Day. India is split, into Hindu India and Muslim Pakistan. Gandhi fasts to end internal violence
1948	Gandhi escapes bomb attack on January 20. On January 30, he is shot and dies. Albert Einstein, famous scientist, says that Gandhi was "a beacon for generations to come"

Index